America in the 1980s and 1990s

By
CINDY BARDEN

COPYRIGHT © 2002 Mark Twain Media, Inc.

ISBN 1-58037-216-3

Printing No. CD-1562

Mark Twain Media, Inc., Publishers
Distributed by Carson-Dellosa Publishing Company, Inc.

Table of Contents

About the American History Series

Welcome to *America in the 1980s and 1990s,* one of the books in the Mark Twain Media, Inc., American History series for students in grades four to seven.

The activity books in this series are designed as stand-alone material for classrooms and home-schoolers or as supplemental material to enhance your history curriculum. Students can be encouraged to use the books as independent study units to improve their understanding of historical events and people.

Each book provides challenging activities that enable students to explore cultural, historical, geographic, and social studies topics. The activities provide research opportunities and promote critical reading, thinking, and writing skills. As students learn about the people and events that influenced history, they will draw conclusions; write opinions; compare and contrast historical events, people, and places; analyze cause and effect; and improve thinking skills. Students will also have the opportunity to apply what they learn to their own lives through reflection and creative writing.

Students can further increase their knowledge and understanding of historical events by using reference sources at the library and on the Internet. Students may need assistance to learn how to use search engines and discover appropriate websites.

Titles of books for additional reading appropriate to the subject matter at this grade level are included at the end of the book.

Although many of the questions are open-ended, an answer key is included for questions with specific answers.

Share a journey through history with your students as you explore the books in the Mark Twain Media, Inc., American History series.

Discovering and Exploring the Americas
Life in the Colonies
The American Revolution
The Lewis and Clark Expedition
The Westward Movement
The California Gold Rush
The Oregon and Santa Fe Trails
Slavery in the United States
The American Civil War
Abraham Lincoln and His Times
The Reconstruction Era
Industrialization in America
The Roaring Twenties and Great Depression
World War II and the Post-War Years
America in the 1960s and 1970s
America in the 1980s and 1990s

Time Line of the 1980s

1980
- Mount St. Helens erupted.
- CNN began broadcasting 24-hour news.
- *Voyager 1* sent back images of Saturn and its moons.
- Ronald Reagan defeated Jimmy Carter for president.
- Smallpox was considered eradicated by the World Health Organization.
- The United States refused to attend the Summer Olympics in Moscow.
- The U.S. Supreme Court allowed patents on living organisms.

1981
- Ronald Reagan was shot by John Hinckley.
- MTV, the 24-hour music station, debuted on cable television.
- 52 American hostages were released from Iran after 14 months.
- Postage rates rose from 15 to 18 cents an ounce.
- Sandra Day O'Connor became the first female Supreme Court Justice.
- The U.S. Agriculture Department tried to classify ketchup as a school lunch vegetable.

1982
- Deaths resulted from poisoned Tylenol™.
- The Equal Rights Amendment failed to be ratified.
- The Vietnam Memorial was erected in Washington, D.C.

1983
- The United States invaded Grenada.
- 40 were killed in the bombing of the U.S. Embassy in Beirut, Lebanon.
- 241 U.S. Marines were killed in the bombing of a barracks in Beirut, Lebanon.
- Vanessa Williams became the first Black Miss America.
- Internet sites got names instead of hard-to-remember numbers.
- Sally Ride became the first American woman in space.
- ZIP+4: 9-digit ZIP codes and postal bar codes were introduced.

1984
- The Soviets and their allies boycotted the Summer Olympics in Los Angeles.
- The AIDS virus was discovered.
- Geraldine Ferraro became the first female vice-presidential running mate for a major party.
- IBM, Sears, and CBS form Prodigy™.
- Portable compact disc players became available.
- The *National Geographic* cover featured a hologram.
- The 3 1/2-inch computer disk drive became available.
- Ronald Reagan was reelected in a landslide election.
- Stonewashed jeans became a national fad.

Time Line of the 1980s (cont.)

1985

- General Motors announced the installation of electronic road maps as an option on some higher-priced car models.
- The Center for Disease Control reported that more than half of all nine-year-olds in the United States showed no sign of tooth decay.
- The *Titanic* wreckage was found and filmed by robotic camera.
- Leaded gasoline was officially banned in the United States.
- The Rock and Roll Hall of Fame opened.

1986

- The Iran-Contra Scandal was reported.
- The television was on more than seven hours a day in average U.S. homes.
- The *Challenger* space shuttle exploded shortly after lift-off.
- Halley's Comet returned.
- U.S. military planes dropped bombs on Libya.
- The Statue of Liberty celebrated its 100th anniversary with a facelift.
- Turner Broadcasting began to colorize black-and-white classic movies.
- The Tax Reform Act of 1986 was passed.

1987

- Half of all U.S. homes with television had cable.
- The world population reached five billion.
- Coca-Cola™ became the #1 soft drink, pushing Pepsi-Cola™ to #2.

1988

- The first transatlantic telephone calls made over fiber-optic lines took place.
- The United States invaded Panama.
- Music CDs outsold vinyl records for the first time.
- 98% of U.S. homes had at least one television set.
- Pan Am Flight 103 exploded over Lockerbie, Scotland; Libyan terrorists were suspected of planting the bomb.
- George Bush was elected president.

1989

- Nintendo™ racked up an annual profit of $1 billion.
- *Voyager 2* sent back images of Neptune.
- Arsenio Hall became the first Black to host a nightly talk show.
- The *Exxon Valdez* oil disaster occurred in Alaska.
- A worldwide ban on ivory was imposed.
- Colin Powell was appointed Chairman of the Joint Chiefs of Staff, the highest army post ever held by a Black officer.
- A major earthquake postponed the third game of the world series between the San Francisco Giants and Oakland Athletics.

Time Line of the 1990s

1990

- Smoking was banned on domestic airplane flights.
- The spotted owl was added to the threatened-species list.
- Dr. Jack Kevorkian became known for assisting patient suicide.
- The Hubble Space Telescope was launched.
- The Clean Air Act was passed.

1991

- The United States bombed Iraq; the Persian Gulf War began.
- The Motion Picture Association reported that only 16% of American movies were fit for those under age 13.
- Courtroom Television Network began broadcasting.
- Three out of four U.S. homes had VCRs.
- Queen Elizabeth II became the first British monarch to address the U.S. Congress.

1992

- 65 million personal computers had been sold to date.
- Riots followed the not-guilty verdict of police officers after the videotaped beating of Rodney King.
- Compact disc music sales passed cassette tape sales.
- The Michelangelo virus disabled computers worldwide.
- Cable television revenues reached $22 billion.
- America Online™ (AOL) reported 200,000 subscribers.
- Bill Clinton defeated Republican incumbent George Bush for president.

1993

- A siege at Waco, Texas, resulted in the deaths of cult members.
- Combat roles became available for women in the U.S. military.
- An explosion at the World Trade Center in New York killed six and trapped tens of thousands.

1994

- Amazon.com™ began selling books online.
- Almost one-third of all American homes had computers.
- The existence of black holes was proved.
- The Whitewater Scandal investigation began.
- A massive earthquake hit Los Angeles.

1995

- O.J. Simpson was found innocent of murdering his ex-wife and her friend.
- Sony™ demonstrated flat-screen television.
- The major U.S. dailies created a national online newspaper network.
- Audio of live events became available on the Internet.
- The bombing at the Oklahoma City federal building killed 168.
- Dr. Bernard A. Harris, Jr., became the first Black American astronaut to walk in space.

Time Line of the 1990s (cont.)

1996
- U.S. athletes won 101 medals at the Summer Olympics in Atlanta, Georgia.
- Two were killed in the Olympic Park bombing.
- Flight 800 from New York crashed, killing all aboard.
- The Unabomber, Theodore Kaczynski, was arrested in Montana.
- More than 100,000 World Wide Web sites were available, and there were 45 million Internet users, including 30 million in the United States.
- The U.S. military barracks in Saudi Arabia were destroyed when a truck bomb exploded outside the barracks, killing 19.

1997
- The first successful clone of an animal was performed in Scotland.
- An IBM computer defeated world chess champion Garri Kasparov.
- Kodak™ produced the first point-and-shoot digital camera.
- Timothy McVeigh was found guilty of the Oklahoma City bombing.
- AOL™ boasted 10 million subscribers.
- 43% of U.S. homes had computers.
- O.J. Simpson was found guilty of wrongful death in a civil suit.

1998
- Apple™ unveiled the colorful iMac™ computer.
- The Unabomber, Theodore Kaczynski, pleaded guilty and accepted life in prison without the chance of parole or the right to appeal.
- The House of Representatives approved the impeachment of President Clinton.
- Two young boys killed five people at a Jonesboro, Arkansas, middle school.
- 1998's summer temperatures were the highest on record.
- John Glenn, veteran astronaut, returned to space at the age of 77 on the space shuttle *Discovery*, becoming the oldest person to travel in space.

1999
- The Senate acquitted President Clinton, and he remained in office.
- A shooting spree at Columbine High School resulted in 15 deaths.
- Viruses continued to attack computers: Melissa, worst to date.
- Great sums were spent to solve Y2K problems.
- An Egyptian air flight crashed off the coast of Nantucket, killing all 217 aboard: cause not determined.
- The Panama Canal was given back to Panama.
- The first nonstop, around-the-world trip in a balloon was completed.
- A Colorado grand jury failed to indict anyone for the murder of 6-year-old Jon-Benét Ramsey.
- Texas Governor George W. Bush, son of former President George H. W. Bush, announced he would run for president in the 2000 primaries.
- By the end of the year, more than 40 million American households were on the Internet.

Name: _____ Date: _____

The 1980s

After the turbulence and struggles of the 1960s and 1970s, Americans were ready for a change. The Vietnam War was finally over. Civil Rights and Women's Rights issues seemed less pressing. People were tired of political protests that at times turned violent.

Sensing the mood of the people, former actor Ronald Reagan ran for president against Jimmy Carter, promising a return to family values, lower taxes, and a reduction in government spending. Elected for two terms, Reagan brought changes and economic prosperity to many Americans.

Fashions went to extremes from the "grunge" look and punk styles of hair and clothing to the conservative suits and haircuts worn by yuppies.

Advances in technology continued at an ever-increasing pace as computers went from the rather simple TRS-80 available in 1980 to much more powerful PCs by the end of the decade. Computers with hard disk drives were first introduced in 1980. By 1981, people could buy laptop computers and solar-powered, hand-held calculators.

Music CDs arrived on the scene in '82, along with the point-and-click computer mouse. By the end of the decade, cell phones, camcorders, and disposable cameras became available.

The 1980s was the decade of arcade games. Atari introduced *Space Invaders*™. Then along came *Pac Man*™ and *Donkey Kong*™. Popular games and toys included Rubik's Cube™, Cabbage Patch™ dolls, Transformers™, and Pictionary™.

The '80s also brought us MTV, CNN, and cable home shopping networks.

Circle "T" for True or "F" for False.

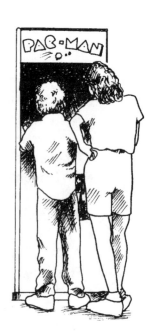

1. T   F   "Grunge" was a popular movie in the '80s.

2. T   F   People began using cell phones in the '80s.

3. T   F   *Space Invaders*™ and *Pac Man*™ were arcade games.

4. T   F   Music CDs first became available in the '80s.

5. T   F   The first computers were available in 1985.

6. T   F   Jimmy Carter defeated Ronald Reagan for president.

Name: _____   Date: _____

Mount St. Helens Erupts

Although Mount St. Helens had not erupted since 1857, residents of southwestern Washington saw warning signs that something was happening inside the volcano early in 1980. A column of magma began pushing up inside the mountain, causing a bulge on the northern face.

An earthquake registering 5.1 caused a landslide on the northern face, taking off the top of the mountain and triggering an eruption on May 18, 1980, at 8:32 A.M.

Forests 17 miles (27 km) away from Mount St. Helens were flattened. Four hundred million tons of dust and gases filled the atmosphere in a cloud 12 miles (19 km) high. Within three days, dust from the blast had traveled as far as the east coast of the United States.

Molten lava flowed hundreds of feet into the valleys surrounding the mountain, causing rushing landslides moving 70 to 150 miles per hour (113–241 kph). The blast killed 57 people and destroyed about 200 square miles (1,518 sq. km) of habitat, including 26 lakes and 150 miles (241 km) of streams. What had once been forests became a grey, desolate, lifeless landscape. Several million fish, birds, and mammals were killed or left homeless.

The eruption caused some of the snow on Mount St. Helens to turn to steam. The rest melted and formed large mudflows that destroyed 200 homes, 27 bridges, and 185 miles (298 km) of road.

The mountain's peak became a crater 1.2 miles (1.93 km) wide and 2.4 miles (3.86 km) long. After the eruption, the elevation of Mount St. Helens decreased from 9,677 feet (2,950 m) to 8,365 feet (2,550 m). A second eruption occurred on May 25. Other smaller eruptions occurred in 1982 and 1986.

1. Use a dictionary. What is lava? _____

   _____

2. Mount St. Helens is still an active volcano. It may erupt again. How would you feel about living in an area near an active volcano?

   _____

   _____

   _____

   _____

   _____

   _____

   _____

   _____

   _____

   _____

Name: _____ Date: _____

Before Reagan Became President

Number the events in Ronald Reagan's early life in order from 1 to 15.

____ A. After his divorce, Reagan dated for a few years and then married another actress, Nancy Davis.

____ B. Ronald Reagan was born in 1911 in a small apartment above a general store in Tampico, Illinois, where his father sold shoes.

____ C. After a screen test in 1937, Warner Brothers offered Reagan a movie contract starting at $200 a week.

____ D. While in the service, he made more than 400 training films.

____ E. His first movie was *Love is on the Air.*

____ F. After graduating from Eureka College in 1932, Reagan worked for a time as a radio sports announcer.

____ G. During the filming of *Brother Rat* in 1938, Reagan met actress Jane Wyman. They were married in 1940.

____ H. During his first year in Hollywood, Reagan acted in seven low-budget films. Gradually, he was offered more important roles and became a popular actor.

____ I. After returning to Hollywood in 1945, Reagan found little work available as an actor.

____ J. In 1942, Reagan enlisted in the Air Force. His poor eyesight kept him from becoming a pilot. Instead, he was assigned to act in military training films.

____ K. When he became president of the Screen Actors Guild in 1947, Reagan worked to improve working conditions, pay, medical insurance, and other benefits for actors.

____ L. Although he did not run for any political office until 1966, Reagan worked on the presidential campaigns of Richard Nixon (1960) and Barry Goldwater (1964).

____ M. In 1949, Ronald and Jane (Wyman) Reagan were divorced.

____ N. He earned money for college by working summers as a lifeguard.

____ O. In 1954, Reagan was hired to host a television program, "General Electric Theater." When the show went off the air eight years later, he became the host of "Death Valley Days."

Name: _____ Date: _____

Shop 'Til You Drop

Malls had become popular in larger cities in the 1970s. By the eighties, they were springing up in cities all across the United States.

Even those who stayed home could partake in another new shopping trend: cable home shopping networks on television. Without leaving home, consumers could purchase a wide variety of items using their credit cards.

Use of credit cards increased dramatically. By the mid-1980s, the average credit card holder carried seven cards. People had a desire to own expensive, fashionable things. They wanted the latest in appliances and electronics. However, more buying resulted in more consumer debt.

Credit cards make it easy for people to buy things they can't afford to pay for at the time of purchase. The minimum monthly payment required is quite small compared to the total amount due. However, the interest rate charged is usually very high. In the long run, people who purchase items with a credit card could easily pay twice the actual cost of an item by the time it is finally paid for.

1. Compare shopping at a mall to buying items through a home shopping television network.

Advantages of Mall Shopping

_____

_____

_____

Advantages of TV Shopping

_____

_____

_____

2. Talk to someone who has ordered something from either a television shopping network or from an Internet site. Ask that person about the experience. Write what he or she liked and disliked about this type of shopping.

Liked: _____

_____

_____

Disliked: _____

_____

_____

3. Why do you think people buy things with credit cards if the items cost so much more in the long run?

_____

_____

_____

Name: _____ Date: _____

The Great Communicator

In college, Ronald Reagan joined the debating team and acted in school plays. After college, he worked as a radio sports broadcaster, then as an actor. His experiences helped him to be a confident, popular speaker, earning him the nickname "The Great Communicator."

At an age when many people begin to think of retirement, Ronald Reagan decided to begin a career in politics. His ability as a speaker helped him get elected as governor of California in 1972.

Four years later, Reagan campaigned for the Republican presidential nomination. He came in a close second to President Gerald Ford who sought reelection.

Not discouraged, he campaigned again in 1980, this time against President Jimmy Carter. Reagan said he was running for those who shared his values of "family, work, neighborhood, peace, and freedom."

During his campaign, Reagan proposed large tax cuts, which he hoped would stimulate the economy and slow inflation. He also wanted to balance the national budget through a drastic cutback on government spending in all areas except defense.

Reagan, with George Bush as his running mate, won the 1980 election by a large margin.

1. Why was Ronald Reagan nicknamed "The Great Communicator"? _____

_____

_____

2. What was his first elected position? _____

3. Who won the presidential election of 1976? _____

4. What values did Reagan believe were important? _____

_____

_____

5. What did Reagan say would be his goals as president? _____

_____

_____

_____

Name: _____ Date: _____

Fads and Fashions of the Eighties

People who wanted to be taken seriously in business or leisure usually wore conservative clothing. In contrast, some teen clothing fads were quite radical. The **punk** style included black clothing, leather jackets, and ripped jeans. Pierced ears, noses, and other body parts were common. Hair dyed bright colors and wild spiky hairstyles became popular.

Another style adopted by young people in the eighties was the "**grunge**" look: oversized, ragged, faded clothing. Black American rap singers influenced fashion by combining the grunge look with sneakers without shoelaces, baseball caps worn sideways or backwards, and sweatsuits.

1. What do you think of kids who pierce their ears, noses, or tongues?

   _____

   _____

2. Would you want to wear punk-style clothing and hairstyles? Why or why not?

   _____

   _____

   _____

3. If you wanted to dye your hair purple, what do you think your parents would say?

   _____

   _____

   _____

4. What clothing or hairstyles do you like that are popular now?

   _____

   _____

   _____

5. If you don't like a current fashion, should you wear it anyway? Why or why not?

   _____

   _____

   _____

Name: _____ Date: _____

Meet the Yuppies

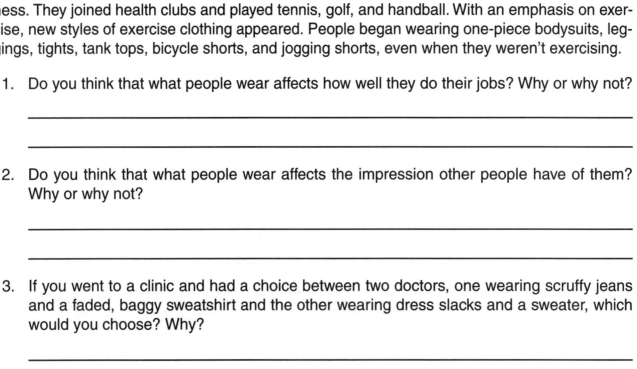

People in the eighties became more focused on earning more money. Recent graduates from college became known as "yuppies" (young urban professionals)—those intent on working long hours to build a successful career and achieve a high standard of living. *Newsweek* magazine called 1984 the "Year of the Yuppie."

More women became interested in having their own professional careers. Many young couples put off having families until they could achieve financial security.

Some yuppies wore dark, conservative clothing and conservative hairstyles. Men and women who wanted to be taken seriously about their careers wore "power suits." Men wore white shirts, silk ties, dark suits, and leather shoes. Women wore white blouses, tailored jackets, and knee-length skirts. Both men and women carried leather briefcases and cellular phones. They wore expensive watches and clothing to show how successful they were.

Even when not on the job, yuppies usually wore expensive clothing like designer jeans, leather shoes, and shirts, jackets, and sweaters with expensive labels.

Concerned about their appearance, yuppies believed in the importance of physical fitness. They joined health clubs and played tennis, golf, and handball. With an emphasis on exercise, new styles of exercise clothing appeared. People began wearing one-piece bodysuits, leggings, tights, tank tops, bicycle shorts, and jogging shorts, even when they weren't exercising.

1. Do you think that what people wear affects how well they do their jobs? Why or why not?

   _____

   _____

2. Do you think that what people wear affects the impression other people have of them? Why or why not?

   _____

   _____

3. If you went to a clinic and had a choice between two doctors, one wearing scruffy jeans and a faded, baggy sweatshirt and the other wearing dress slacks and a sweater, which would you choose? Why?

   _____

   _____

Name: _____ Date: _____

Reaganomics and Foreign Affairs

President Reagan's economic policies tended to be conservative, favoring the interests of big business and the wealthy. He reduced or ended many federal programs in an effort to cut government expenses. If the government spent less money, taxes would be lower.

Reagan believed that if taxes were lower, people, especially the wealthy, would invest more money in corporations. As a result, businesses would prosper, producing more jobs and higher wages for workers. He claimed this would create a "trickle-down" effect that would help poor people.

Referred to as "**Reaganomics**," his policies were extremely popular among many, including yuppies and business people. They believed this would help the nation achieve a new level of prosperity. Others criticized him for ending programs to help needy people.

Foreign affairs became another major focus of the Reagan administration. The president took a strong stand against terrorism in 1983 by sending 800 U.S. soldiers as part of an international peacekeeping effort to Lebanon where Christians and Muslims were at war.

Reagan called the Soviet Union a "great evil" and believed it was necessary to prevent the spread of communism. In 1983, he also sent 1,900 U.S. soldiers to Grenada, an island in the Caribbean to prevent the Cuban government from establishing a communist government there.

Relations between the United States and Libya were also tense because of Libya's support of terrorist groups. In 1986, Reagan sent U.S. military planes in a surprise attack on two Libyan cities.

During his second term as president, Reagan met with Soviet leader Mikhail Gorbachev. The two leaders signed a treaty reducing the number of nuclear missiles and decreasing the tension between the two countries.

1. What is your opinion of "Reaganomics"?

   _____

   _____

   _____

   _____

2. Do you think the United States should get involved in the politics of other governments? Why or why not?

   _____

   _____

   _____

   _____

   _____

Name: _____ Date: _____

Vice President George Bush

In the 1980 presidential primary elections, George Bush campaigned against Ronald Reagan for the Republican nomination. At the national convention, Reagan was chosen as the Republican candidate. Although they had been opponents in the primary race, Reagan asked Bush to be his vice-presidential running mate. They defeated President Jimmy Carter by over 13 million popular votes.

As vice president, Bush asked for more responsibility, and Reagan agreed. Bush met with the president on a regular basis and became his advisor and confidant.

Vice President Bush traveled to 59 foreign countries on behalf of the Reagan administration. As head of the Task Force for Regulatory Relief, he recommended ways to cut paperwork in government agencies. He also led another task force whose aim was to stop illegal drug smuggling in south Florida.

Both Reagan and Bush were very popular with the public and easily won reelection in 1984.

When Reagan needed surgery for cancer in 1985, he signed a document transferring presidential power to Bush to take effect when the anesthesia was administered; Bush then officially became acting President of the United States. On the following day, Reagan signed a second letter reclaiming his power and duties. While Reagan recuperated, Bush continued to perform the daily routine duties of the president.

1. Use a dictionary. What does *confidant* mean?

   _____

   _____

   _____

Write your answers on your own paper.

2. According to the U.S. Constitution, the only official duties of the vice president are to preside over the Senate and vote in the event of a tie. What other duties do you think a vice president should have?

3. Many people have considered the vice president as an unimportant position. Do you think it is important? Why or why not?

4. Do you think it is important that the nation not be without a president, even for a short time? Why or why not?

Name: _____ Date: _____

'80s Trivia

- President Jimmy Carter decided the United States would not participate in the 1980 Summer Olympic games held in Moscow to protest Russia's invasion of Afghanistan. Sixty-five other countries joined the boycott. Four years later, the Soviet Union and its allies refused to attend the Summer Olympic games in Los Angeles.

- The first IBM-PCs became available in 1981 at a cost of $4,500. More than 65,000 units sold in the first four months. By 1982, 5.5 million PCs had been sold.

- The one-button point-and-click mouse became available in 1982.

- *E.T.: The Extra-Terrestrial* broke all box office records in 1982 by surpassing the $100 million mark of ticket sales in the first 31 days after it opened.

- "M*A*S*H" became the most watched television program in history when an estimated 125 million people tuned in for the final episode in 1983.

- While testing the microphone before his weekly radio broadcast on August 10, 1984, President Ronald Reagan joked, "My fellow Americans, I am pleased to tell you that I just signed legislation that would outlaw Russia forever. We begin bombing in five minutes." Reagan didn't know that technicians had the microphone open, and his words were being broadcast.

- Chinese television launched a weekly half-hour program of old Donald Duck and Mickey Mouse cartoons in 1986.

- Game three of the 1989 World Series between the San Francisco Giants and the Oakland Athletics was canceled when an earthquake measuring 7.1 struck the San Francisco Bay area.

- President Reagan liked jelly beans. As governor and president, he always kept a jar of jelly beans on his desk.

- Kellogg's™ of Battle Creek, Michigan, stopped tours of their breakfast cereal plant in 1986. They felt that company secrets were at risk from spies from other cereal manufacturers.

1. Use reference sources. Write two other interesting bits of trivia about the 1980s.

_____

_____

_____

_____

Name: _____ Date: _____

If You Were Alive in '85

If you were alive in 1985 …

… you could have seen the largest sand castle in the world near St. Petersburg, Florida. The castle was four stories tall and contained hidden treasure for kids who came in and demolished the work of art, with permission, a week after it was built.

… you could have used one of the first car cell phones.

… you might have used the new Microsoft Windows 1.0 operating system on your computer.

… you could have heard television broadcasts in stereo.

… you could have purchased a Sony™ radio the size of a credit card.

… you could have been one of the first to join America Online™.

… you might have played the new *Super Mario Brothers*™ computer game.

… you could have tried New Coke™ … but not for long. It was quickly replaced with Classic Coke™.

… you would have paid 22 cents for a first-class stamp.

… you could have visited baby Shamu at Sea World in Orlando, Florida. Shamu was the first killer whale to survive after being born in captivity.

1. Talk to a friend or relative who remembers events from 1985. Ask that person to tell you about his or her memories from the mid-eighties. Write about these memories on your own paper and share them with the class.

Name: _____ Date: _____

Then and Now

Read the statements about 1986. Add a statement about how things are the same or different today.

1. **Then:** The Wrigley Company raised the price of its seven-stick pack of Wrigley's™ chewing gum from a quarter to 30 cents. It was the first time the price of chewing gum had risen in six years.

   Now: _____

   _____

   _____

2. **Then:** Martin Luther King, Jr.'s, birthday became a public holiday in the United States, celebrated on the third Monday in January.

   Now: _____

   _____

   _____

3. **Then:** FOX became the fourth major U.S. television network, joining ABC, CBS, and NBC.

   Now: _____

   _____

   _____

4. **Then:** Cable shopping networks began broadcasting.

   Now: _____

   _____

   _____

5. **Then:** The hottest fashions for young people in 1986 included miniskirts, tie-dyed shirts, and bleached jeans.

   Now: _____

   _____

   _____

   _____

Name: _____ Date: _____

The *Challenger* Tragedy

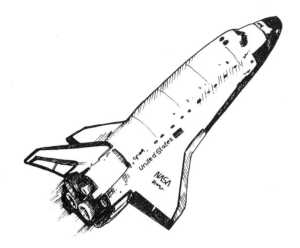

In the early 1980s, NASA's space shuttle program was very active. By the end of 1985, 24 missions had been successfully completed.

In January 1986, NASA prepared to send *Challenger* into space. For the first time, one member of the crew was not a trained astronaut. She was Christa McAuliffe, a history teacher.

Seventy-three seconds after takeoff from the Kennedy Space Center, the U.S. space shuttle *Challenger* exploded, killing everyone on board.

President Reagan formed a special commission to investigate the cause of the accident and develop corrective measures. They found the disaster had been caused by the failure of a sealing ring in one of the shuttle's solid-fuel rockets. Faulty design of the seal and the unusually cold weather had allowed hot gases to leak through. Flames inside the booster rocket escaped and burned through the shuttle's external fuel tank. Liquid hydrogen and liquid oxygen fuels mixed and began to burn, causing the shuttle to tear apart.

The commission also claimed officials at NASA had allowed the launch to take place in spite of concerns voiced by NASA engineers.

Following the *Challenger* disaster, the shuttle launch program was halted for two years until the commission's investigation was completed and designers had made several modifications. NASA implemented stricter regulations for quality control and safety.

Christa McAuliffe had been chosen to join *Challenger's* crew from among 11,000 applications to NASA's Teacher in Space Program. She planned to teach two classes from space, keep a journal of her trip, and use that information to tour the country teaching students about the space program.

In her application, she wrote, "I would like to humanize the Space Age by giving the perspective of a non-astronaut. I think the students will look at that and see that an ordinary person is contributing to history. If they can make that connection, they are going to be excited about history."

1. Explain what you think Ms. McAuliffe meant and why you agree or disagree.

_____

_____

_____

_____

_____

_____

Name: _____ Date: _____

Believe It or Not

- In the early eighties, Americans became obsessed with the Rubik's Cube™, a complex puzzle invented in the 1970s by Erno Rubik, a Hungarian professor. By the end of 1981, more than 10 million had been sold. The idea was to turn the 26 smaller cubes so that one solid color showed on each side of the cube. Since there are more than 43 quintillion different positions, many people became frustrated with this puzzle. As a result, more than 100,000 Cube Smashers™ were also sold.

- On July 2, 1982, Larry Walters tied 42 weather balloons to a lawn chair and flew as high as 16,000 feet before shooting the balloons with a pellet gun and landing about 90 minutes later. The FAA fined him $1,500.

- George Plimpton played an April Fool's joke on readers in 1985 when he wrote an article published in *Sports Illustrated* about Sidd Finch, a 28-year-old aspiring monk who could throw a 168 mph fastball. He claimed Finch was a free-agent pitcher in the New York Mets' spring training camp who had learned to pitch while playing the French horn in his spare time. Plimpton later admitted that Finch was not a real person.

- 1985 was one second longer than most years. One "leap second" was added by the world's official clock to compensate for the gradual slowing of the Earth's rotation. The practice continues every few years on New Year's Eve.

- If you went to the Ringling Brothers and Barnum & Bailey Circus in 1985, you might have seen four "unicorns" on display. However, inspectors determined the animals were goats with surgically implanted horns. They ordered the circus to quit advertising the fake unicorns as anything but goats.

- The Coca-Cola Company made a showy, glitzy announcement in 1985, that it was changing its 99-year-old secret formula, calling New Coke™ "the most significant soft drink development" in the company's history. The new product was a gigantic flop. Consumers refused to buy New Coke™. They preferred "The Real Thing," the original Coca-Cola™. Coca-Cola Company executives relented and returned to the old formula with a new name: Classic Coke™.

1. Do you think people really believed they were seeing unicorns? Why or why not?

_____

_____

_____

Name: _____ Date: _____

The Iran-Contra Scandal

In 1981, President Reagan had directed the Central Intelligence Agency (CIA) to help guerilla forces in Nicaragua overthrow Daniel Ortega's Sandinista government. Soldiers fighting against the communist government of Nicaragua were called Contras.

In 1986, details of what became known as the Iran-Contra scandal came to light. High-ranking members of the Reagan administration had arranged for the secret sale of arms to Iran, in direct violation of current U.S. laws. Profits from the $30 million in weapons sales were channeled to the Contras to supply them with arms for use against the Sandinista government—also a violation of U.S. policy.

The chief negotiator of these deals was Lieutenant Colonel Oliver North, a military aide to the National Security Council, who set up a covert network to provide the Contras with their own ships, airplanes, airfields, and secret bank accounts.

Following investigations by the Tower Commission in 1987, a report censured President Reagan and his advisors for not controlling the actions of the National Security Council.

Although the commission claimed the president had the ultimate responsibility for implementation of his administration's policies, they found no firm evidence that he had known about the diversion of funds to the Contras.

Oliver North

Colonel North was tried and convicted of obstructing Congress and unlawfully destroying government documents, but his conviction was later overturned.

A final report in 1994 concluded that although there was no evidence that Reagan had broken the law, the president may have participated in, or known about, a cover-up.

1. Use a dictionary. What does *guerilla* mean? _____

   _____

2. Use a dictionary. Define *censure.* _____

   _____

3. Do you think a president has the right to break a law or allow others to do so, even if he believes the results are justified? Why or why not?

   _____

   _____

   _____

   _____

Name: _____ Date: _____

In the News in 1987

The purpose of a headline is to catch the readers' attention. Use six words or less to write a newspaper headline for each item.

1. _____

Bobro, a huge barge, set sail from New York with 3,200 tons of garbage. The floating trash heap began an eight-week, 6,000-mile trip in search of a willing dumping site. *Bobro* returned to New York Harbor after the lengthy journey and brought all that garbage back with it.

2. _____

Statistics showed that the median age when American men first got married rose to 25.5 years.

3. _____

A 15,000-mile, four-year trek ended for Steve Newman in 1987 when he became the first man to walk solo around the world.

4. _____

Eleven-year-old John Kevin Hill landed his plane at National Airport in Washington, D.C. He became the youngest aviator to fly across the United States.

5. _____

According to government sources, the combined local, state, and national debt rose to $10,047 per person in the United States. The federal debt alone amounted to $7,650 per person.

6. _____

For the first time, Paramount Home Video placed a commercial at the front of a new video release, "Top Gun." The 30-second Diet Pepsi™ ad reduced the price of the video to consumers by $3.

7. _____

On October 19, 1987, the largest stock market drop in Wall Street history occurred on "Black Monday" when the Dow Jones Industrial Average fell 508.32 points, losing 22.6% of its total value. This far exceeded the one-day loss of 12.9% that began the Great Depression following the great stock market crash of 1929.

Name: _____ Date: _____

George Herbert Walker Bush

Use reference sources to complete this activity. Fill in the circle for the correct answer to each question.

1. George Bush grew up in what state?

   ○ Florida   ○ Massachusetts   ○ Texas   ○ California

2. Shortly after graduating from high school, Bush joined the service and trained to be a pilot. What branch of service did he join?

   ○ Army   ○ Navy   ○ Air Force   ○ Marines

3. Where did Bush attend college after World War II ended?

   ○ Yale   ○ Harvard   ○ Texas A & M   ○ Florida State

4. At what sport did Bush excel in college?

   ○ soccer   ○ basketball   ○ football   ○ baseball

5. In 1966 and 1968 Bush was elected to the U.S. House of Representatives from what state?

   ○ Florida   ○ Massachusetts   ○ Texas   ○ California

6. Bush was defeated for election to the U.S. Senate. Instead, he was appointed as U.S. Ambassador to the United Nations. He then served as chairman of the Republican National Committee. Which president appointed Bush to these positions?

   ○ Richard Nixon   ○ Ronald Reagan   ○ Gerald Ford

7. Before he became vice president in 1981, George Bush was a diplomat in what country?

   ○ Sweden   ○ China   ○ Vietnam   ○ Canada

8. George Bush served as director of the _____.

   ○ FBI   ○ NRA   ○ CIA   ○ IRS   ○ EPA   ○ DNR

9. Who was president when George Bush was vice president?

   ○ Ronald Reagan   ○ Richard Nixon   ○ Jimmy Carter

10. Who was vice president when Bush was president?

    ○ Bill Clinton   ○ Walter Mondale   ○ Dan Quayle

Name: _____ Date: _____

What If?

1. What if you had been a child during the 1980s? How would your life be different from what it is today?

_____

_____

_____

_____

2. What if you had been an athlete in 1980 who had been training for the Summer Olympics in Moscow? How would you have felt when you learned the president had decided that the U.S. would not participate?

_____

_____

_____

_____

3. What if you could meet anyone who was famous during the 1980s or 1990s? Who would you most like to meet, and why?

_____

_____

_____

_____

4. Write a "what if?" question about the 1980s and answer it.

Question: _____

_____

_____

_____

Answer: _____

_____

_____

_____

23

Name: _____ Date: _____

Review a Box Office Hit

Watch one of these movies that was popular in the 1980s and write a review. Explain what you liked and didn't like about the movie and your recommendation for the reader of your review.

1980 *Elephant Man*   *Star Wars: The Empire Strikes Back*

1981 *Indiana Jones and the Raiders of the Lost Ark*   *Chariots of Fire*

1982 *Gandhi*   *E.T.: The Extra-Terrestrial*

1983 *Stars Wars: Return of the Jedi*   *The Right Stuff*

1984 *Gremlins*   *Indiana Jones and the Temple of Doom*
          Ghostbusters   *Amadeus*

1985 *Out of Africa*   *Back to the Future*

1986 *Top Gun*   *Crocodile Dundee*

1987 *The Last Emperor*   *Raising Arizona*
          Three Men and a Baby

1988 *Rain Man*   *Gorillas in the Mist*

1989 *Driving Miss Daisy*   *Batman*
          Field of Dreams   *Indiana Jones and the Last Crusade*
          Dead Poet's Society   *Little Mermaid*

My review of _____.

_____

_____

_____

_____

_____

_____

_____

_____

_____

Name: _____ Date: _____

President George Bush

After serving eight years as vice president, George Bush ran for president in 1988. Bush promised to veto any increases in taxes. "Read my lips. No new taxes," he stated. He also promised to cut the capital gains tax and continue Reagan's defense programs. Bush opposed gun control and abortion.

After winning the election, Bush became a very active, popular president. He signed the Americans with Disabilities Act in 1990 to reduce legal and physical obstacles to people with disabilities. He worked to increase federal programs for education, child care, and technological research and development. Bush signed a bill to improve the nation's interstate highway system. He also signed the Clean Air Act, setting higher standards for air quality and cleaner burning fuels.

Bush's plans to help the troubled savings and loan industry backfired, however, when more than a thousand savings and loan associations went bankrupt due to poor banking practices, poor government regulation, and corruption.

In December 1989, Bush sent 24,000 troops to Panama to help overthrow President Manuel Noriega who had been indicted for drug trafficking; U.S. officials claimed he had lost the 1989 election for president.

Working with Soviet leader Mikhail Gorbachev, Bush launched plans to reduce U.S. troops in Europe and move the Soviet Union toward a democratic form of government.

When Iraq invaded Kuwait in 1990, Bush formed a coalition of 30 nations and sent troops to the region, freeing Kuwait.

While successful in areas of foreign policy, Bush's attempts to balance the budget and reduce the national debt without raising taxes met resistance in Congress. When he ran for reelection in 1992, he was defeated by Bill Clinton.

Mikhail Gorbachev and George H.W. Bush

1. Which of Bush's achievements do you think were the most important?

_____

_____

_____

2. Why? _____

_____

_____

_____

Name: _____ Date: _____

The Eighties: Causes and Effects

A **cause** is an event that produces a result. An **effect** is the result produced. For each cause, write an effect.

1. People became very frustrated when they were unable to solve the Rubik's Cube™ puzzle.

    Effect: _____

    _____

    _____

2. President Carter decided that U.S. athletes would not participate in the 1980 Summer Olympic games in Moscow.

    Effect: _____

    _____

    _____

3. The U.S. sold weapons to Iran and used the profits to support the Contras in Nicaragua.

    Effect: _____

    _____

    _____

4. President Reagan appointed a commission to study the explosion of the space shuttle *Challenger.*

    Effect: _____

    _____

    _____

5. Ronald Reagan asked George Bush to be his vice-presidential running mate in 1980.

    Effect: _____

    _____

    _____

6. Mount St. Helens erupted.

    Effect: _____

    _____

    _____

Name: _____ Date: _____

What Happened When?

Use the time line on pages 2 and 3 to complete this activity.

1. What percentage of U.S. homes with TV had cable in 1987? _____

2. What three corporations joined to form Prodigy™? _____
   _____

3. In what year did Halley's Comet return? _____

4. Who was the president in 1987? _____

5. In what year did CNN begin broadcasting news 24 hours a day, seven days a week?
   _____

6. Who was the first American woman in space?
   _____

7. What percent of American homes had television in 1988?
   _____

8. What was featured on the cover of *National Geographic* magazine in 1984?
   _____

9. What item was banned worldwide in 1989? _____

10. Which car company was the first to install electronic road maps as an option in luxury cars?
    _____

11. When was the sale of leaded gasoline banned in the United States? _____

12. Which amendment failed to become part of the U.S. Constitution in 1982? _____
    _____

13. How much did it cost to mail a letter in 1981? _____

14. Which happened first: the dedication of the Vietnam Memorial or the discovery of the wreckage of the *Titanic*?
    _____

15. Which came first, the U.S. invasion of Panama or the U.S. invasion of Grenada?
    _____

Name: _____ Date: _____

Eighties Scavenger Hunt

To complete this scavenger hunt, use the Internet and other reference sources to find the answers.

1. George H. W. Bush announced that he did not like one particular vegetable and had decided he would never eat it again.

   What vegetable did George Bush dislike? _____

2. In 1989, this country changed its name to Myanmar.

   What was its former name? _____

3. The video game *Pac Man*™ was invented in Japan in the late seventies and came to U.S. arcades in 1982. The name of the game was based on the Japanese word *paku.*

   What does *paku* mean? _____

4. In 1980, the *Ladies' Home Journal* featured a man on its cover for the first time in its 97-year history.

   Who was the man? _____

5. The first U.S. space shuttle was launched on April 12, 1981.

   What was the name of this space shuttle? _____

6. The first artificial heart transplant took place in 1982.

   A. What was the patient's name? _____

   _____

   B. How long did he live? _____

   C. Who performed the surgery? _____

   Artificial Heart

   _____

7. 264,000 bottles of a pain reliever were recalled in 1982 after a California man was poisoned. Seven people died of cyanide poisoning from taking pills that had been deliberately tampered with.

   What was the name of the pain reliever? _____

8. As an actor, Ronald Reagan was best remembered for his role as football star George Gipp.

   What was the name of the movie? _____

   _____

Name: _____ Date: _____

Review the 1980s

Write the answers in the blanks.

Christa McAuliffe	**George H. W. Bush**	**John W. Hinckley**
Martin Luther King, Jr.	**Mount St. Helens**	**Oliver North**
Ronald Reagan	**Rubik's Cube™**	**Shamu**
unicorns	**E. T.**	**yuppies**

_____ 1. Vice president when Reagan was president

_____ 2. A frustrating toy popular in the 1980s

_____ 3. Hoax created by the Ringling Brothers and Barnum & Bailey Circus

_____ 4. Popular movie that broke all box office records in 1982

_____ 5. Volcano that erupted in 1980 in Washington state

_____ 6. People in the eighties who focused on earning more money by working long hours to build a successful career and achieve a high standard of living

_____ 7. Name of the first killer whale to survive after being born in captivity

_____ 8. His birthday became a public holiday celebrated on the third Monday in January

_____ 9. When elected, he was the oldest man to become President of the United States.

_____ 10. Man who shot President Reagan

_____ 11. Person convicted of wrongdoing in the Iran-Contra Scandal

_____ 12. Teacher killed when the space shuttle *Challenger* exploded

Name: _____ Date: _____

Who's Who?

Women's Liberation continued to be an important issue in the eighties and nineties, and many American women made breakthroughs in sports, medicine, politics, art, science, and other fields.

Use reference sources if you need help matching these women with their areas of fame.

A. First woman appointed Attorney General
B. Mayor of Chicago
C. First Black female astronaut in space
D. First female Supreme Court Justice
E. First female police chief of a major city, Portland, Oregon
F. Olympic gymnast and medal winner
G. Secretary of Health and Human Services
H. First woman appointed Secretary of State
I. Vice-presidential candidate
J. Surgeon General
K. U.S. Ambassador to Czechoslovakia
L. Winner of three 1988 Olympic gold medals in track

Madeleine Albright

_____ 1. Mary Lou Retton

_____ 2. Geraldine Ferraro

_____ 3. Sandra Day O'Connor

_____ 4. Shirley Temple Black

_____ 5. Jane Byrne

_____ 6. Penny Harrington

_____ 7. Dr. Mae C. Jemison

_____ 8. Madeleine Albright

_____ 9. Janet Reno

_____ 10. Jocelyn Elders

_____ 11. Donna Shalala

_____ 12. Florence Griffith-Joyner

Florence Griffith-Joyner

Name: _____ Date: _____

Math Facts

1. The 26 smaller cubes of the popular Rubik's Cube™ sold in the eighties have 43 quintillion different possible combinations.

   Write the number 43 quintillion. _____

2. In 1997, nearly 8 out of every 10 U.S. public schools had Internet access.

   Write the percent for 8 out of 10. _____

3. In 1981, postage rates rose from 15 to 18 cents an ounce.

   What was the percent of increase in rates? _____

4. In 1984, airlines installed the first public telephones for passengers to use while flying across the United States. A three-minute call cost $7.50. Each additional minute cost $1.25.

   How much would a 10-minute call have cost? _____

5. In 1987, the U.S. budget reached the trillion dollar mark.

   Write one trillion dollars in numbers. _____

6. In 1998, Americans averaged 2,300 phone calls a year.

   A. How many did they average per week? _____

   B. How many did they average per day? _____

7. Ask your family to keep track of the number of calls made at work and at home for one week.

   How many calls did members of your family make in one week? _____

8. Born in February 1911, Ronald Reagan took the oath of office as President of the United States in January 1981.

   How old was he when he became president? _____

9. After Mount St. Helens erupted in 1980, the elevation of the mountain decreased from 9,677 to 8,365 feet.

   How much shorter was Mount St. Helens after it erupted? _____

10. IBM-PCs sold for $4,500 in 1981. Check several ads for personal computers.

    Is the cost for a PC higher or lower than it was in 1981? _____

Name: _____ Date: _____

Environmental News

Events during the eighties and nineties brought about renewed concerns for the environment and endangered species.

Select one of the environmental topics below. Use reference sources to answer the questions on your own paper.

1. On March 24, 1989, the Exxon oil tanker *Exxon Valdez* ran aground on a reef. About 240,000 barrels of crude oil (11 million gallons) spilled into the waters off the coast of Alaska.

   → What caused the oil tanker to run aground?
   → Why did it take so long to clean up the oil spill?
   → What was the effect of this incident on plants and animals?

2. When the spotted owl was added to the threatened species list in 1990, it sparked controversy between loggers and conservationists.

   → Where do spotted owls live?
   → What caused the destruction of their habitat?
   → Why did conservationists and logging companies battle over the fate of the spotted owls?
   → What is the current status of the spotted owl?

3. The last wild California Condor was taken into captivity in 1987 in an attempt to increase the numbers of the species through a captive breeding program. Considered the most endangered species of bird in the United States, there were only 27 of these magnificent birds alive at that time.

   → Why did California Condors nearly become extinct?
   → How successful has the breeding program been?
   → How many California Condors are now living?

4. The hole in the ozone layer, first detected in 1977, was thoroughly documented and caused great concern to environmentalists by the mid-eighties.

   → What caused the hole in the ozone layer?
   → What effect does the hole in the ozone layer have on life on Earth?

5. Africanized honey bees, aggressive honey bees that escaped from Brazil, were first discovered in the United States in the border town of Hidalgo, Texas, in October 1990. They later spread throughout all of the Southwestern United States.

   → What had made them so aggressive?
   → Why is that a problem?
   → What is being done about it?

Name: _____ Date: _____

Changes and Innovations in the '90s

As the 1990s began, Americans were optimistic about relations with other countries. With the collapse of the Berlin Wall and the breakup of the Soviet Union, the Cold War had finally ended. People in the United States felt there was a possibility of peace with the former communist countries. Unfortunately, that optimism was short-lived as the problems in the Middle East increased.

Troubling events marred the peace as the threat of terrorism became more real with the bombing of the World Trade Center in New York, the bombing of the Murrah Federal Building in Oklahoma City, and a series of shooting rampages in schools. Americans realized that terrorist attacks could and did occur in the United States.

During the latter part of the 1980s, the United States had experienced the greatest economic boom since World War II. The nineties were a prosperous period for most Americans. Unemployment and inflation remained low for much of the decade.

The constantly quickening pace of technological changes, in particular the development of the Internet, provided new and exciting sources of information and communication.

Episodes of racial violence, particularly the riots after the trial of four White police officers for brutally beating Rodney King, showed that in spite of progress, severe problems still existed.

Hot toys in the '90s included Toobers & Zots™, Furbies™, the Tamagotchi™ "virtual pet", and anything related to Teenage Mutant Ninja Turtles™ or Power Rangers™. By the end of the decade, most children were infected with "Pokemon™ fever," and both young and old began collecting Beanie Babies™.

Interview someone who was born before 1980. Ask that person to tell you what he or she remembers best about the 1990s.

_____

_____

_____

_____

_____

_____

_____

_____

Name: _____ Date: _____

Americans Travel the Information Superhighway

Probably the most amazing innovation of the 1990s was the widespread availability of the Internet. People called it the Information Superhighway—a way to travel across the world of cyberspace.

With a computer, modem, and telephone line, people could connect with computers all over the world. They could access data, read newspapers or magazines, and find financial, legal, or medical advice.

In addition to a new way of accessing information, the Internet also provided new ways to communicate. Sending e-mail became more convenient and sometimes less expensive than making telephone calls or using "snail mail." People could send and receive e-mail messages any time of the day or night.

Internet chat rooms became popular. People with similar interests or concerns could exchange information or simply "talk" with each other online.

The Internet also provided new services. Sites like ebay.com helped individuals with items to sell to reach potential buyers.

Companies began to advertise and sell online. Customers could check out items on website catalogs and order almost anything from groceries to medications to automobiles—without ever leaving home.

As the Internet provided more options for banking, paying bills, and purchasing online, privacy and security became an important issue.

1. Do you think "Information Superhighway" is a good description of the Internet? Why or why not?

   _____

   _____

   _____

2. Use a reference source if needed. What does the "e" in e-mail mean?

   _____

3. What do you like most about the Internet?

   _____

   _____

4. What do you like least about the Internet?

   _____

   _____

Name: _____ Date: _____

Operation Desert Storm

In 1990, Iraqi leader Saddam Hussein sent troops to invade and occupy Kuwait to gain control of more of the oil resources in the Middle East. This presented a threat to Saudi Arabia, a U.S. ally and the region's leading oil producer. Hussein was also developing nuclear, chemical, and possibly biological weapons.

Understanding the threat of Hussein and the importance of oil to the U.S. economy, President George Bush stated, "This aggression will not stand." He compared Hussein to Adolf Hitler.

A coalition of 30 nations joined in a buildup of more than half a million troops in the region. Bombing of Iraq began in January 1991, followed by a ground invasion in February, which quickly ended the invasion of Kuwait. Before leaving, Iraqi troops set fire to Kuwaiti oil fields. More than 150,000 Iraqi soldiers and civilians died in the brief Persian Gulf War. Fewer than 200 Allied troops were killed.

However, Saddam Hussein remained in power and continued to be a source of problems for the rest of the decade.

Use reference sources to identify the following Middle East countries. Place the number of the country next to its name in the list below.

_____ A. Bahrain

_____ B. Cyprus

_____ C. Iran

_____ D. Israel

_____ E. Jordan

_____ F. Kuwait

_____ G. Lebanon

_____ H. Oman

_____ I. Qatar

_____ J. Saudi Arabia

_____ K. Syria

_____ L. United Arab Emirates

_____ M. Yemen

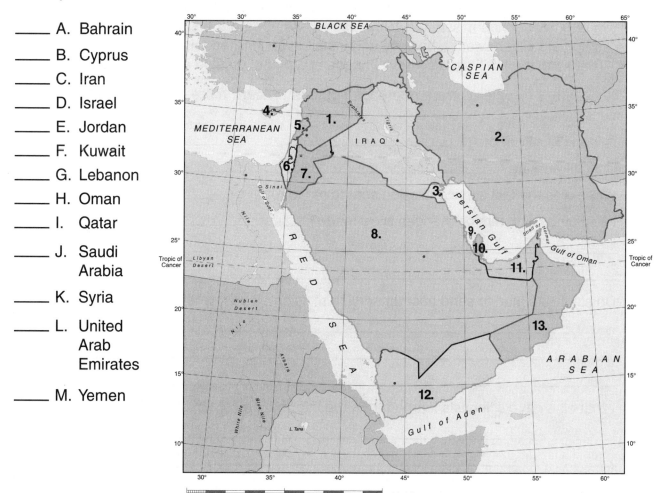

Name: _____ Date: _____

The Hubble Space Telescope

At a cost of $1.5 million, NASA launched the Hubble Space Telescope (HST) in 1990 with high expectations of success from the first orbiting observatory. Once in orbit, however, one of the mirrors was discovered to be incorrectly ground, resulting in blurred pictures.

In 1993, a crew on the space shuttle *Endeavor* went into orbit on a successful service mission to make repairs.

The HST has provided data for calculating the rate at which galaxies are moving away from the Milky Way and for the number of galaxies in the universe. This information can be used to calculate the age of the universe.

Scientists announced in June 1994 that the HST had provided the first convincing evidence of the existence of a black hole, which had been purely theoretical up until this point.

The detailed images of Jupiter, provided by the HST when fragments of the comet Shoemaker-Levy 9 collided with the planet in 1994, allowed scientists to analyze the chemical make-up of Jupiter's atmosphere.

In another service mission in 1997, astronauts aboard the shuttle *Discovery* replaced some equipment with newer technology and installed an infrared telescope.

Thanks to the HST, we also have images of a planet outside our solar system.

Use the Internet or other current reference sources to learn more about the Hubble Space Telescope.

1. Is the HST still in orbit? _____

2. Is it still working? _____

3. When was the last service mission sent to make repairs? _____

4. What type of repairs or changes were made? _____

_____

_____

5. Do scientists plan to send another service mission? If yes, when and why?

_____

_____

_____

6. What else have scientists learned from the information sent by the HST?

_____

_____

Name: _____ Date: _____

Not Guilty Verdict Leads to Riots

Although great strides had been made in civil rights prior to the nineties, racial tension in many parts of the country remained high.

On March 3, 1991, on a Los Angeles freeway, two California Patrol officers clocked a car at speeds of over 110 miles per hour. The lengthy pursuit was ended by blocking the path of the car driven by Rodney King, whose blood-alcohol level was two and a half times the legal limit. When stopped, King resisted arrest and pushed away officers. Force was used and King was very badly beaten. An observer videotaped the arrest and beating and sent the tape to a local television station. The tape was broadcast around the world, calling attention to police brutality in Los Angeles.

All charges against King were dropped four days later.

A commission appointed by the mayor of Los Angeles documented the use of excessive force and racial harassment by the Los Angeles Police Department.

In spite of graphic videotape evidence, the four police officers were found not guilty of criminal charges in 1992. When the verdict was announced, it resulted in one of the worst race riots in U.S. history in Los Angeles. By the time the riots were over, more than 40 people had been killed, thousands had been arrested, hundreds of structures had been destroyed by fire, and nearly $1 billion in property damage had occurred.

1. What do you think would have been your reaction if you had seen the video on the news?

_____

_____

_____

2. Why do you think the charges against Rodney King were dropped?

_____

_____

_____

3. Do you think the not-guilty verdict justified rioting? Why or why not?

_____

_____

_____

Name: _____ Date: _____

Not Guilty Verdict Leads to Riots (cont.)

No charges were filed against nearly 20 other police officers who had watched the beating. While they had not participated, they had taken no action to stop it.

1. Do you think charges should have been filed against them? Why or why not?

_____

_____

_____

A second trial convicted two of the officers of criminally violating Rodney King's civil rights. The judge sentenced them to 30 months in prison.

2. What is your opinion of the sentence of 30 months in prison?

_____

_____

_____

3. What punishment do you think would have been appropriate for the police officers involved?

_____

_____

_____

A panel of three judges of the Ninth Circuit Court of Appeals reversed the sentence on the grounds that this was too lenient, claiming the sentence should have been about six years. After reviewing the case, the United States Supreme Court sent the case back to the lower courts for resentencing. However, the trial judge reimposed the original sentences.

Rodney King filed a civil suit against the city of Los Angeles, the Los Angeles Police Department, and the officers. The city of Los Angeles conceded liability. The jury awarded Rodney King $3.8 million to compensate him for loss of work, medical costs, and pain and suffering.

4. What is your opinion of the result of the civil suit against the city of Los Angeles?

_____

_____

_____

_____

Name: _____ Date: _____

William Jefferson Blythe III

William Jefferson Blythe III was born in Hope, Arkansas, in 1946, three months after his father had died in a car accident. For a few years, Bill and his mother lived with her parents.

When Bill was four, his mother married Roger Clinton. They moved to Hot Springs, Arkansas, and had a second son in 1956. Although he hadn't been adopted by his stepfather, Bill began using his last name; he had his name legally changed in 1962.

Because of Roger Clinton's problems with alcohol and violent behavior, Bill's mother divorced him in 1962 but remarried him three months later.

Bill Clinton played saxophone in the high school band, in a jazz trio, and in the all-state band. In 1963, his classmates elected him to attend the "Boys State" National Convention in Washington, D.C. Clinton graduated fourth in his class of 363.

While attending Georgetown University from 1964 to 1968, Clinton worked at various part-time jobs to help pay for his education. He earned a Rhodes Scholarship, which paid for his expenses to attend Oxford University in England for two years. In 1970, he entered Yale University Law School where he met Hillary Rodham, his future wife. Bill and Hillary were married in 1975.

After earning his law degree in 1973, Clinton taught at the University of Arkansas. Although he lost an election for Congress the following year, he was elected attorney general of Arkansas in 1976 and governor of Arkansas two years later.

Put these events from Bill Clinton's early life in chronological order from earliest to most recent.

_____ A. Clinton attended Yale.

_____ B. William Jefferson Blythe III was born.

_____ C. Clinton was elected attorney general of Arkansas.

_____ D. Clinton taught at the University of Arkansas.

_____ E. William Blythe changed his last name to Clinton.

_____ F. Clinton lost an election for Congress.

_____ G. Clinton went to college in England.

_____ H. Clinton's father died in a car accident.

_____ I. Clinton earned his law degree.

_____ J. Clinton became the governor of Arkansas.

_____ K. Clinton attended Georgetown University.

_____ L. Bill and Hillary were married.

Name: _____ Date: _____

Tragedy in Waco, Texas

Members of a cult called the Branch Davidians lived in a compound in Waco, Texas. Their origin can be traced to the Davidian movement that began in California in 1934. Members believed the end of the world was near and would be preceded by catastrophe and war.

In Waco, Texas, members lived a communal life, studied the Bible, recruited new members, and prepared for the coming apocalypse by stockpiling food, weapons, fuel, and other supplies.

When federal officials tried to arrest their leader, David Koresh, for possession of illegal firearms on February 28, 1993, he and his followers began shooting, killing four agents and wounding 12 others. Several Branch Davidian members were also killed or wounded.

As a result, federal agents surrounded the compound and waited, hoping those inside would surrender. After a 51-day standoff, agents pumped tear gas into the compound and stormed it with armored vehicles. A fire broke out in the compound, killing 86 men, women, and children.

Some people blamed the government for invading a private religious group and using excessive violence. The government claimed the fire had been started by cult members who preferred to die rather than surrender. Some survivors believed the compound had caught fire as a result of the assault.

Use a dictionary:

1. Define *communal*. _____

_____

2. Define *apocalypse*. _____

_____

3. How would you feel if your family decided to join a commune like the Branch Davidians or another type of survivalist group?

_____

_____

_____

4. Give suggestions on other ways federal officials might have handled the situation that may have prevented the loss of lives.

_____

_____

_____

_____

Name: _____ Date: _____

What Do You Think?

1. In 1991, the U.S. Supreme Court ruled that a sentence of life imprisonment for drug possession may be cruel, but is not unusual; thus, it does not violate the Eighth Amendment's prohibition against cruel and unusual punishment.

   Do you agree or disagree? Why? _____

   _____

   _____

   _____

2. In 1993, a Florida judge ruled that it was legal for a child to divorce his or her biological parents. The court case involved a 12-year-old boy who didn't want his parents anymore.

   What is your opinion? _____

   _____

   _____

   _____

3. People have different opinions about the Internet.

   A. The Internet and e-mail bring people closer together.

   B. People spend so many hours alone on computers that the Internet keeps people apart.

   Which opinion do you agree with? Why? _____

   _____

   _____

   _____

4. A raft carrying six-year-old Elian Gonzales, his mother, stepfather, and ten other refugees from Cuba capsized off the coast of Miami. Due to the death of his mother at sea, an international custody battle for the boy began.

   Do you think the boy should have been allowed to stay with relatives in the United States, or do you think it was right for him to be sent back to live with his father in Cuba? State reasons for your opinion.

   _____

   _____

   _____

   _____

Name: _____ Date: _____

President Bill Clinton's First Term

During the 1992 presidential campaign, Bill Clinton promised to lower taxes for middle-class Americans and to make affordable healthcare a top priority.

In his inauguration speech in January 1993, Clinton said, "To renew America we must be bold. We must do what no generation has had to do before. We must invest more in our own people, in their jobs, and in their future, and at the same time cut our massive debt."

It became obvious almost immediately after he took office that Clinton wouldn't be cutting taxes for middle-class Americans. He claimed he had no idea how great the federal deficit was until he became president. A tax cut would add to the debt and hurt the economy.

As promised, Clinton made healthcare a top priority. He appointed his wife, Hillary Rodham Clinton, to head a commission to develop a plan to reform healthcare. In September 1993, the Clinton healthcare plan was introduced to Congress. If approved, every American would be covered by health insurance. Due to the high cost of the program and opposition by many different groups, including private insurance companies, the plan failed.

While president, Clinton appointed many women and members of minorities to his Cabinet and other important positions.

One of the most controversial laws President Clinton signed was the Brady Law. It required a five-day waiting period for people purchasing handguns so background checks could be made.

Clinton also signed the Family and Medical Leave Act, which made it illegal to fire someone for taking time off to care for a member of the immediate family who was ill.

Another law Clinton signed to reform the welfare system put a time limit on federal benefits to unemployed welfare recipients.

1. Why do you think some people felt Clinton had made a false promise about cutting taxes just to get elected?

_____

_____

2. Do you think the Family and Medical Leave Act is a good law? Why or why not?

_____

_____

3. Do you think the welfare time limit legislation is a good law? Why or why not?

_____

_____

Name: _____ Date: _____

Compare and Contrast

In 1993, statistics showed that one in three Americans was doing some work at home instead of driving to a job.

1. What are some advantages of working at home?

   _____

   _____

   _____

2. What are some disadvantages of working at home?

   _____

   _____

   _____

3. Which do you think would be better? Give reasons for your opinion.

   _____

   _____

   _____

Compare using the Internet and using books for research.

4. What are the advantages of using books?

   _____

   _____

   _____

5. What are the advantages of using the Internet?

   _____

   _____

   _____

6. Which do you prefer? Why?

   _____

   _____

   _____

   _____

Name: _____ Date: _____

Controversies Plague Bill Clinton

Many controversies arose during Bill Clinton's first term and carried into his second four years as president.

Vince Foster, a boyhood friend and Clinton's personal lawyer, committed suicide in 1993. Critics claimed Hillary Clinton had removed files from his office that could have been damaging to the Clintons. Accusations were even made that Foster had been murdered, and the Clintons were involved. Investigations into the matter failed to find evidence.

In 1978, the Clintons had invested money in a resort in Arkansas named Whitewater. When the resort went bankrupt, the Clintons lost money. Investigations to determine if they were guilty of illegal financial deals failed to find evidence of wrongdoing.

In 1994, Paula Jones publicly charged Bill Clinton with sexual harassment. Clinton denied the charges, claiming nothing illegal or inappropriate had happened.

Although these and other unresolved issues hung over Clinton's head, he was elected to a second term in November 1996.

Shortly after he was reelected, another scandal erupted. The Democrats were accused of raising campaign funds illegally and accepting money from foreign citizens and businesses. Critics claimed that by donating money to elect the president, those nations could influence his foreign policies.

Kenneth Starr, who had been appointed in 1994 to investigate the Whitewater deal, continued to investigate other areas of the Clintons' lives. By 1998, Starr's investigation had cost the public over $40 million and hadn't proven anything; yet, he continued to expand his investigation to include unrelated issues.

The charges by Paula Jones against Clinton were dismissed in 1998 but were reopened after an appeal by her lawyers. The case was settled with Clinton agreeing to pay Paula Jones $850,000. Then, Clinton was accused of another improper relationship with a White House intern, Monica Lewinsky.

The combination of charges, accusations, and unanswered questions prompted the House of Representatives to open an inquiry to determine if the charges were serious enough to require impeachment.

1. How do you think you would have felt if you had been Bill Clinton?

    _____

    _____

    _____

    _____

2. How do you think you would have felt if you had been Bill Clinton's wife or daughter?

    _____

    _____

    _____

    _____

Name: _____ Date: _____

Bombers Strike America

The destruction of the World Trade Center in New York City on September 11, 2001, was not the first terrorist attack on the United States, nor was it the first time terrorists had targeted the twin towers of the World Trade Center.

An explosion in New York City on February 26, 1993, killed six people, injured more than a thousand, and trapped tens of thousands of office workers when a van packed with a 1,210-pound bomb exploded in the parking garage underneath the World Trade Center. The explosion left a gigantic crater 200 feet wide and caused over $591 million in damage. Four Muslim fundamentalists were convicted and sentenced to prison.

Another unbelievable tragedy occurred in 1995 when Timothy McVeigh used a powerful truck bomb to blow up the Alfred P. Murrah Federal Building in Oklahoma City, killing 168 men, women, and children. Millions watched live coverage as workers tried to assist the hundreds of injured.

New York City's World Trade Center

Before being captured in 1996, the Unabomber, Theodore Kaczynski, killed three people and injured 29 others with homemade letter bombs. He believed technology would destroy the world; to prevent this, he had targeted people he considered a threat.

These and other incidents made Americans aware that terrorism and tragedy could happen in the United States.

1. Do you think the U.S. government has done enough to prevent terrorism? Why or why not?

   _____

   _____

   _____

2. What do you think is the most important safety precaution that is being taken or should be taken?

   _____

   _____

   _____

3. Use reference sources to learn more about the events of September 11, 2001, or one of the 1990s incidents listed above. Write a short report on your own paper. Answer the questions *who, what, when, where, why,* and *how*.

Name: _____ Date: _____

Report on the News

Use what you learned about one of the topics below to write a newspaper article. Use the Internet or other reference sources for additional information. Use your own paper if you need more room.

In your article, be certain to answer the questions *who, what, when, where, why*, and *how*.

Topics:

The Eruption of Mount St. Helens
The *Challenger* Tragedy
The Iran-Contra Scandal
Operation Desert Storm
The 1992 Riots in Los Angeles
The Tragedy in Waco, Texas
The Bombing in Oklahoma City
The Shooting in Littleton, Colorado

Headline: _____

Article: _____

_____

_____

_____

_____

_____

_____

_____

_____

_____

_____

_____

_____

_____

_____

_____

_____

_____

_____

Name: _____ Date: _____

The End of Affirmative Action

In the 1960s, Affirmative Action began as a way to increase opportunities for minorities by giving them preference for hiring, promotions, and college admissions. Richard Nixon was the first president to implement federal Affirmative Action policies. From the beginning, Affirmative Action was very controversial.

1. Read the two opinions of the issue. Write your opinion of Affirmative Action and the reasons for your answer.

   Against: Policies that give preferred treatment based on membership in a group are against the Constitutional belief that all people are created equal. It causes reverse discrimination against qualified people who are not a member of a minority because of discrimination in the past against minorities.

   For: Affirmative Action is the only way to provide everyone with equal opportunities in jobs, promotions, education, and other benefits. Discrimination in the past has made it necessary to open up opportunities traditionally closed to women and members of minorities.

   _____

   _____

   _____

   _____

   _____

In a White House memo on Affirmative Action, President Clinton called for the elimination of any program that "(a) creates a quota; (b) creates preferences for unqualified individuals; (c) creates reverse discrimination; or (d) continues even after its equal opportunity purposes have been achieved."

California passed a state ban on all forms of Affirmative Action in 1997. Proposition 209 stated that "the state shall not discriminate against, or grant preferential treatment to, any individual or group on the basis of race, sex, color, ethnicity, or national origin in the operation of public employment, public education, or public contracting."

After being in effect for over 25 years, many people felt Affirmative Action programs were no longer necessary.

2. What do you think? _____

   _____

   _____

   _____

Name: _____ Date: _____

Take a Survey

In 1995, the average U.S. home had nearly six radios.

How many radios do you and your family own? _____

Take a survey. Ask 20 people how many of each type of electronic device they have in their homes. Record your results on the chart.

	Radios	TVs	Cellular Telephones	Computers	VCRs and CD/DVD Players
1					
2					
3					
4					
5					
6					
7					
8					
9					
10					
11					
12					
13					
14					
15					
16					
17					
18					
19					
20					
Total					

What is the average number of electronic devices owned per family in the group you surveyed?

Average number of radios: _____

Average number of TVs: _____

Average number of cell phones: _____

Average number of VCRs and CD/DVD players: _____

Average number of computers: _____

Name: _____ Date: _____

Violence in Schools

Within a two-year period in the nineties, there were five major shootings in U.S. schools. Other violent incidents in schools caused grave concern about the safety of students.

The worst incident took place on April 20, 1999, at Columbine High School in Littleton, Colorado. Two students went on a shooting rampage, killing 12 students and one teacher before killing themselves.

The two students, Dylan Klebold and Eric Harris, belonged to a group called the Trench Coat Mafia. They had spent much of their spare time before the incident playing violent video games.

Their motives for the shooting are unknown. Perhaps they were unable to tell the difference between the virtual world of computer games and reality. Maybe they simply wanted to become famous. No one will ever know for sure.

1. What safety precautions are taken at your school?

   _____

   _____

   _____

2. Do you believe the safety precautions at your school are good enough? Why or why not?

   _____

   _____

   _____

3. What do you think is the biggest problem in your school?

   _____

   _____

   _____

4. What is your opinion of what is being done about it?

   _____

   _____

   _____

5. If you knew a student who bragged about having a gun or threatened to shoot someone, what would you do?

   _____

   _____

   _____

Name: _____ Date: _____

The Impeachment of President Clinton

Accused of sexual harassment by one woman, President Clinton lied under oath about his involvement with another woman to the grand jury in 1998. He later made a public apology to the nation for lying.

According to the U.S. Constitution, impeachment of the president means the U.S. House of Representatives accuses him of "treason, bribery, or other high crimes and misdemeanors." The president may be removed from office after a trial and a two-thirds vote by the U.S. Senate.

On October 8, 1998, the House of Representatives voted to open an impeachment inquiry against President Clinton. The main question became whether the charges were serious enough to require impeachment. The decision to proceed came in December.

Because at the time he lied he was under oath, Clinton was impeached on two charges: perjury and obstruction of justice.

Many people felt that what Clinton did was wrong but that the president's personal life wasn't anyone else's business, and the charges were not severe enough to remove him from office.

A few hours before President Clinton gave his State of the Union speech on January 19, 1999, a trial began in the Senate to determine if Clinton would remain president. To be convicted of the charges, two-thirds of the Senators would have to vote that he was guilty on either charge.

After a five-week trial, the Senate voted 55 not guilty on the first charge and 50–50 on the second one. Clinton remained president.

1. Use a dictionary. What does *perjury* mean? _____

   _____

2. Do you think perjury and obstruction of justice should be considered "high crimes and misdemeanors"? Why or why not?

   _____

   _____

   _____

3. Do you think the president or any public official should be accountable to the public for what he or she does in private if it is not illegal? Why or why not?

   _____

   _____

   _____

4. How many of the 100 Senators would have had to vote guilty for Clinton to be removed from office?

   _____

Name: _____ Date: _____

Who Would You Interview?

You are a reporter for a magazine in January 1999. Your boss wants you to write a personal article about Bill or Hillary Clinton and his or her reaction to the impeachment charges.

Who would you rather interview? _____

Write 12 questions you could ask the president or first lady during an interview to prepare an article for your paper.

1. _____

   _____

2. _____

   _____

3. _____

   _____

4. _____

   _____

5. _____

   _____

6. _____

   _____

7. _____

   _____

8. _____

   _____

9. _____

   _____

10. _____

    _____

11. _____

    _____

12. _____

    _____

Name: _____ Date: _____

The Hullabaloo About Y2K

As the year 2000 approached, people began to predict all kinds of disasters, from the end of the world to the collapse of civilization. Some feared the failure of all technology at midnight on New Year's Eve, which would cause planes to fall from the sky, massive power failures, and the collapse of worldwide financial and distribution systems. Even scarier was the idea that missiles armed with nuclear warheads might be automatically launched due to computer error.

Some people withdrew large amounts of cash and stocked up on canned goods and other supplies. Survivalists took guns and supplies and sought safety in remote areas.

One real problem that needed to be dealt with was computer programming that had been written ten or more years earlier and hadn't been updated. Without reprogramming, the date on computers would go from 1999 to 1900 rather than 2000. Billions of dollars were spent worldwide on Y2K upgrades of computer software.

In a bank, this type of computer error would affect the calculation of interest on all loans and savings accounts. In business, a failure of the computer to show the correct date could affect production and shipping schedules. A computer system that calculated benefits for people based on age or years of service would totally fail if the current year were not correct.

As people welcomed the New Year in a worldwide celebration, none of the predictions for disaster occurred.

1. Why do you think so many people believed that disasters might happen at the end of 2000?

_____

_____

_____

2. Why do you think people stockpiled food, cash, weapons, and supplies?

_____

_____

_____

3. If you believed society was going to collapse in six months; all communications, technology, and transportation systems would be disrupted; there would be massive power failures; and all banks and the stock market would fail, what would you do to prepare?

_____

_____

_____

Name: _____ Date: _____

The Nineties: Causes and Effects

A **cause** is an event that produces a result. An **effect** is the result produced. For each effect, write a possible cause.

Cause	Effect
_____ _____ _____ _____ _____	1. People stocked up on canned goods, water, and money before January 1, 2000.
_____ _____ _____ _____ _____	2. Affirmative Action is no longer a federal policy.
_____ _____ _____ _____	3. A fire broke out in the Branch Davidian compound in Waco, Texas, killing 86 men, women, and children.
_____ _____ _____ _____	4. Riots broke out in Los Angeles in 1992.
_____ _____ _____ _____	5. The United States joined other nations in sending troops to Kuwait and bombing Iraq.

Name: _____ Date: _____

Review the 1990s

Match the person or term on the right with the appropriate statement on the left.

_____ 1. Branch Davidian leader

_____ 2. President who was impeached

_____ 3. Orbiting observatory launched by NASA

_____ 4. Iraqi leader who invaded Kuwait

_____ 5. Man videotaped being beaten by police officers

_____ 6. City where race riots occurred in 1992

_____ 7. Site of Branch Davidian Compound

_____ 8. Six-year-old refugee from Cuba

_____ 9. Appointed by President Clinton to head a commission to develop healthcare reform

_____ 10. Resort in Arkansas that went bankrupt

_____ 11. Site of bombing by Muslim fundamentalists in 1993

_____ 12. Building destroyed by a truck bomb in Oklahoma City

_____ 13. Attorney who investigated charges against President Clinton

_____ 14. Lying under oath

_____ 15. Great disaster; end of the world

A. Elian Gonzales

B. Hillary Clinton

C. World Trade Center

D. Bill Clinton

E. Whitewater

F. Waco, Texas

G. Rodney King

H. Saddam Hussein

I. David Koresh

J. apocalypse

K. perjury

L. Hubble Space Telescope

M. Alfred P. Murrah Federal Building

N. Kenneth Starr

O. Los Angeles

Write "F" for fact or "O" for Opinion

_____ 16. President Clinton should have been found guilty and removed from office.

_____ 17. Affirmative Action programs favored hiring and promoting and other opportunities for members of minorities.

_____ 18. President Clinton was elected for two terms.

_____ 19. Ronald Reagan was a better president than Bill Clinton.

_____ 20. Riots create more problems than they solve.

Name: _____ Date: _____

Nineties Scavenger Hunt

Use the Internet or other reference sources to find the answers to these questions.

1. When it opened in Minnesota in 1992, it was the largest mall in the United States.

   What was its name? _____

2. Computer-generated dinosaurs roamed Earth for the first time in this popular 1993 Steven Spielberg movie.

   What was the name of the movie? _____

3. The 1994 movie *Forrest Gump* used digital photo tricks to insert the main character into historical footage.

   Which presidents did Forrest Gump meet? _____

4. The Rock and Roll Hall of Fame Museum opened in 1995.

   Where is it located? _____

5. J.K. Rowling published the first Harry Potter book in 1998.

   What was the title of the book? _____

6. In 1998, two Major League baseball players beat the home run record set by Roger Maris in 1961. Sammy Sosa hit 66 home runs, but another player did even better; he hit 70 homers.

   What was the player's name? _____

7. "Tiger" Woods became the youngest winner of the U.S. Junior Amateur Golf Championship in 1991.

   "Tiger" is a nickname. What is his first name? _____

8. The first successful clone of an animal was performed by scientists in Scotland in 1997. The animal's name was Dolly.

   What type of animal was Dolly? _____

9. The leader of the Branch Davidians in Waco, Texas, changed his name to David Koresh.

   What was his name before he changed it? _____

10. Who was the Hubble Space Telescope named after? _____

11. What was that person's occupation? _____

12. Who was the first Black woman to become a commercial airline pilot captain?

   _____

Name: _____ Date: _____

Read All About It!

Option 1: Read a fiction or nonfiction book about the 1980s or 1990s.
Option 2: Read a biography of someone who played a role in history during the 1980s or 1990s.
Option 3: Read one of the books that received the Newbery Award between 1990 and 1999. (See the list on the following page.)

Title and author of the book: _____

Was the book fiction or nonfiction? _____

What years were covered in the book? _____

Briefly describe the main character. _____

_____

_____

Where did the main character live? _____

_____

Summarize two major events described in the book. _____

_____

_____

_____

_____

_____

What was the major problem the main character had to face? _____

_____

_____

_____

How was that problem resolved? If it wasn't resolved, why not? _____

_____

_____

Did you like the book? Why or why not? _____

_____

_____

The 1990s Newbery Award Winners

1999 Winner: *Holes* by Louis Sachar
Honor Book: *A Long Way from Chicago* by Richard Peck

1998 Winner: *Out of the Dust* by Karen Hesse
Honor Books: *Ella Enchanted* by Gail Carson Levine
Lily's Crossing by Patricia Reilly Giff
Wringer by Jerry Spinelli

1997 Winner: *The View from Saturday* by E.L. Konigsburg
Honor Books: *A Girl Named Disaster* by Nancy Farmer
The Moorchild by Eloise Jarvis McGraw
The Thief by Megan Whalen Turner

1996 Winner: *The Midwife's Apprentice* by Karen Cushman
Honor Books: *What Jamie Saw* by Carolyn Coman
Yolonda's Genius by Carol Fenner
The Great Fire by Jim Murphy

1995 Winner: *Walk Two Moons* by Sharon Creech
Honor Books: *Catherine, Called Birdy* by Karen Cushman
The Ear, the Eye, and the Arm by Nancy Farmer

1994 Winner: *The Giver* by Lois Lowry
Honor Books: *Crazy Lady!* by Jane Leslie Conly
Dragon's Gate by Laurence Yep
Eleanor Roosevelt: A Life of Discovery by Russell Freedman

1993 Winner: *Missing May* by Cynthia Rylant
Honor Books: *What Hearts* by Bruce Brooks
Somewhere in the Darkness by Walter Dean Myers

1992 Winner: *Shiloh* by Phyllis Reynolds Naylor
Honor Books: *Nothing But the Truth: A Documentary Novel* by Avi
The Wright Brothers: How They Invented the Airplane by Russell Freedman

1991 Winner: *Maniac Magee* by Jerry Spinelli
Honor Book: *The True Confessions of Charlotte Doyle* by Avi

1990 Winner: *Number the Stars* by Lois Lowry
Honor Books: *The Winter Room* by Gary Paulsen
Afternoon of the Elves by Janet Taylor Lisle
Shabanu, Daughter of the Wind by Suzanne Fisher Staples

History Projects

Complete one of these projects. Work alone, with a partner, or with a small group if appropriate.

- Create a detailed time line of the 1980s or 1990s with illustrations and maps.

- Make a videotape of an interview with a rock star or rock group of the '80s. Be sure to dress the part.

- Do a detailed comparison between any two of the men who were president in the 1980s and/or 1990s. Include the ways in which they were alike and the ways in which they were different.

- Make a scrapbook about Operation Desert Storm. Add captions for all pictures. You can download pictures from the Internet, photocopy them from books, or draw your own.

- Write articles for one page of a newspaper dated any time between 1980 and 1999.

- Write and illustrate a poem about the eighties or nineties. Read your poem to the group.

- Learn and demonstrate a dance popular in the 1980s. Teach others to do the dance.

- Write a detailed report about the conditions in your city or community during the 1980s or 1990s. Include copies of local newspaper articles.

- Create a journal that could have been written by someone between 1980 and 1990 describing everyday life and events. Include at least five entries for each year.

- Prepare and present a 10-minute speech either in favor of or against the impeachment of President Clinton.

- Prepare a detailed biography of one of the presidents or first ladies who lived in the White House during the 1980s or 1990s.

- Make a chart showing details of important environmental events and legislation during the '80s and '90s.

- Do a complete history of the development of computers between 1980 and 1999.

- Prepare a skit using the action figures of Power Rangers™, Teenage Mutant Ninja Turtles™, or characters from the Pokemon™ series.

Learn More About …

Select one of the topics or one of the people listed below who had an impact on American history during the 1980s or 1990s. Use the Internet and other reference sources to write a three- to five-page report with illustrations.

Nancy Reagan

People

Madeleine Albright
Jim Bakker
Guion Bluford
Barbara Pierce Bush
George H. W. Bush
Jane Byrne
Jimmy Carter
Rosalynn Carter
Hillary Rodham Clinton
William J. Clinton
Jocelyn Elders
Geraldine Ferraro
Bill Gates
Florence Griffith-Joyner
Penny Harrington
Jesse Jackson
Dr. Mae C. Jemison
Rodney King
Oliver North
Sandra Day O'Connor
Colin Powell
Nancy Davis Reagan
Ronald Reagan
Janet Reno
Donna Shalala
H. Norman Schwarzkopf

Topics

The Iran-Contra Affair
Operation Desert Storm
The Whitewater Scandal
The Los Angeles riots of 1992
Reaganomics
The space program in the 1980s
    and 1990s
The development of the Internet
The Hubble Space Telescope
Nancy Reagan's "Just Say No" program
Barbara Bush's literacy program
Hillary Clinton's healthcare proposal

H. Norman Schwarzkopf

Bill Gates

Geraldine Ferraro

Suggested Reading

Barbara Bush: First Lady of Literacy by June Behrens

George Bush: Forty-First President of the United States by June Behrens

Ronald Reagan: An All-American by June Behrens

The Impeachment of William Jefferson Clinton by Daniel Cohen

Timelines: 1980s by Jane Duden and Gail B. Stewart

The 1980s: From Ronald Reagan to MTV by Stephen Feinstein

The 1990s: From the Persian Gulf War to Y2K by Stephen Feinstein

Mister President: The Story of Ronald Reagan by Mary Virginia Fox

Bill Clinton by Elaine Landau Franklin

William J. Clinton: Our Forty-Second President by Graham Gaines

Barbara Pierce Bush by Judith E. Greenberg

Bill & Hillary: Working Together in the White House by Keith Elliot Greenberg

George Bush by Zachary Kent

Ronald Reagan by Zachary Kent

Ronald Reagan: Our Fortieth President by Cynthia Klingel and Robel B. Noyed

Geraldine Ferraro: The Woman Who Changed American Politics by Don Lawson

The Picture Life of Ronald Reagan by Don Lawson

The Picture Life of George Bush by Ron Schneiderman

Bill Clinton by Michael A. Schuman

Hillary Rodham Clinton by Victoria Sherrow

Jesse Jackson: I Am Somebody by Charman Simon

Ronald Reagan by George Sullivan

Jesse Jackson: Still Fighting for the Dream by Brenda Wilkinson

Answer Keys

The 1980s (p. 6)

1. F   2. T   3. T   4. T
5. F   6. F

Mount St. Helens Erupts (p. 7)

1. lava: melted rock that comes out of a volcano onto the earth's surface

Before Reagan Became President (p. 8)

A. 13	I. 10
B. 1	J. 8
C. 4	K. 11
D. 9	L. 15
E. 5	M. 12
F. 3	N. 2
G. 7	O. 14
H. 6	

The Great Communicator (p. 10)

1. He was a confident, popular speaker.
2. Governor of California
3. Jimmy Carter
4. family, work, neighborhood, peace, freedom
5. to cut taxes, decrease government spending, and balance the national budget

Vice President George Bush (p. 14)

1. confidant: a trusted person with whom one can share secrets; a close friend

The Iran-Contra Scandal (p. 20)

1. guerilla: a member of a small group engaged in sabotaging, harassing, or raiding who is not part of the regular military
2. censure: a judgment or resolution condemning a person for misconduct; specifically, an official expression of disapproval passed by a legislature

George Herbert Walker Bush (p. 22)

1.	Massachusetts	2.	Navy
3.	Yale	4.	baseball
5.	Texas	6.	Richard Nixon
7.	China	8.	CIA
9.	Ronald Reagan	10.	Dan Quayle

What Happened When? (p. 27)

1. 50%
2. Sears, IBM, and CBS
3. 1986
4. Ronald Reagan
5. 1980
6. Sally Ride
7. 98%
8. a hologram
9. ivory
10. General Motors
11. 1985
12. The Equal Rights Amendment
13. 18 cents
14. Dedication of the Vietnam Memorial in 1982
15. Grenada

Eighties Scavenger Hunt (p. 28)

1. broccoli   2. Burma
3. eat   4. Robert Redford
5. the *Columbia*
6A. Barney Clark   6B. 112 days
6C. Dr. William DeVries   7. Tylenol™
8. *Knute Rockne—All American*

Review the 1980s (p. 29)

1. George H. W. Bush
2. Rubik's Cube™   3. unicorns
4. E. T.   5. Mount St. Helens
6. yuppies   7. Shamu
8. Martin Luther King, Jr.
9. Ronald Reagan   10. John W. Hinckley
11. Oliver North   12. Christa McAuliffe

Who's Who? (p. 30)

1. F 2. I 3. D 4. K
5. B 6. E 7. C 8. H
9. A 10. J 11. G 12. L

Math Facts (p. 31)

1. 43,000,000,000,000,000,000
2. 80%
3. 20%
4. $16.25
5. $1,000,000,000,000
6A. 44.2
6B. 6.3
7. Answers will vary.
8. 69: one month short of his 70th birthday
9. 1,312 feet
10. Answer will depend on current PC prices.

Americans Travel the Information Superhighway (p. 34)

2. electronic

Operation Desert Storm (p. 35)

A. 9	H. 13
B. 4	I. 10
C. 2	J. 8
D. 6	K. 1
E. 7	L. 11
F. 3	M. 12
G. 5	

The Hubble Space Telescope (p. 36)

Answers will vary depending on current information.

William Jefferson Blythe III (p. 39)

A. 6	G. 5
B. 2	I. 7
C. 11	J. 12
D. 8	K. 4
E. 3	L. 10
F. 9	H. 1

Tragedy in Waco, Texas (p. 40)

1. communal: living with a group and sharing housing, food, work, child care, money, etc.
2. apocalypse: worldwide disaster; end of the world

The Impeachment of President Clinton (p. 50)

1. perjury: lying while under oath at a trial
4. 67

Review the 1990s (p. 54)

1. I 2. D 3. L 4. H
5. G 6. O 7. F 8. A
9. B 10. E 11. C 12. M
13. N 14. K 15. J 16. O
17. F 18. F 19. O 20. O

Nineties Scavenger Hunt (p. 55)

1. Mall of America
2. *Jurassic Park*
3. John F. Kennedy, Lyndon Johnson, and Richard Nixon
4. Cleveland, Ohio
5. *Harry Potter and the Sorcerer's Stone* (*Harry Potter and the Philosopher's Stone* in the U.K.)
6. Mark McGwire
7. Eldrick
8. a sheep
9. Vernon Howell
10. Edwin P. Hubble
11. astronomer
12. Melissa Ward